Poised in Power

Harnessing Confidence Through Self-Care

Way, Inc.
Prosper, Texas

Harnessing Confidence Through Self-Care

Dedication

To all the dreamers who believe in the boundless potential of their aspirations, this book is for you. Your unwavering determination and unshakeable belief in yourself inspire us all.

For the resilient souls who have weathered storms and emerged stronger, this journal is your companion. Your courage and tenacity are the true embodiments of power.

To those who understand that confidence is a journey, not a destination, this work is a guide. Your commitment to growth and self-care is the foundation upon which greatness is built.

In the pages of this journal, we celebrate your audacity to reach for the stars, your dedication to self-improvement, and your unyielding pursuit of confidence and power.

May these words empower you, guide you, and remind you that you are, indeed, *Poised for Power*. Your potential is limitless, and your journey is just beginning.

With unshakable confidence and unwavering determination, let us embark on this transformative voyage together. Your path to empowerment awaits.

Poised for Power: Harnessing Confidence Through Self-Care, is a testament to the relentless spirit of those who refuse to be held back, who choose to rise above, and who dare to be unstoppable.

Self-care is not an act of indulgence, but a dialogue of respect; it's the soul whispering to the universe, 'I am my own greatest commitment.

Introduction

Welcome to the transformative journey of *Poised for Power: Harnessing Confidence Through Self-Care*, a guided journal designed to empower you to unlock your fullest potential through prioritizing your self-care. Within these pages, you will embark on a remarkable expedition towards a more confident, poised, and powerful version of yourself.

In a world that constantly demands more from us, where self-doubt can often eclipse our inner radiance, it's time to reclaim your self-confidence and harness the incredible power that resides within you. This journal is your trusted companion on this exhilarating voyage towards unshakable confidence, renewed self-esteem, and genuine self-care.

We live in a time where confidence is not just a desirable trait; it's an indispensable asset. Whether you're striving for career success, nurturing fulfilling relationships, or pursuing personal growth, confidence is the cornerstone of your journey to achievement. But confidence is not an innate quality; it's a skill that can be cultivated and refined through deliberate actions and self-care practices.

Poised for Power is not just another journal; it's your roadmap to self-discovery and empowerment. We've carefully crafted this journal to guide you through a series of purposeful exercises, empowering prompts, and insightful reflections that will help you:

Unearth Your Inner Strength: *Dive deep into your thoughts, feelings, and aspirations to discover the incredible reservoir of potential within you.*

Nurture Self-Compassion: *Learn to treat yourself with the kindness and compassion that you deserve, dismissing self-criticism and doubt from your life.*

Cultivate Self-Care Rituals: *Develop a personalized self-care regimen that renews your energy, fosters resilience, and ignites your confidence.*

Set Bold Goals: *Define your dreams, set audacious goals, and devise a strategic plan to achieve them.*

Celebrate Achievements: *Cultivate a habit of recognizing and celebrating your accomplishments, no matter how big or small.*

We are thrilled to accompany you on this empowering journey. Together, we will unravel the layers of self-doubt, insecurities, and limiting beliefs that have held you back for far too long. You will emerge from this guided journal with a newfound sense of self-assurance, ready to conquer your aspirations with unwavering confidence.

Are you ready to unlock the boundless potential that has always been within you? Are you ready to harness your inner power and claim the success, happiness, and fulfillment you deserve? If your answer is a resounding "yes," then let's embark on this extraordinary adventure together, for you are ***Poised for Power!***

Self-Care Ain't Selfish, It's Essential

Dive deep into the heart of human potential, and you'll uncover a golden truth. At our core lies an unwavering strength, waiting to be harnessed. And the secret key to this treasure? It's the transformative art of continuous and intentional self-care.

Self-care is not a buzzword, nor is it a fleeting trend. It's an age-old philosophy, a sacred ritual, and most importantly, it's a necessity. Think of it as the fuel that powers the engine of our very existence. When we speak of self-care, we're not just talking about indulgent spa days or luxurious vacations (though they certainly have their place). We're talking about a holistic, encompassing approach that nourishes the mind, body, and soul. It's the deliberate act of showing up for yourself, of declaring that you are worth the time and effort.

Why is self-care essential? Because it's intricately linked to the pillar of confidence. A tree, no matter how mighty, can only stand tall when its roots are deep and well-fed. Similarly, our confidence, our ability to believe in ourselves, to stand our ground, and to shine — stems from how well we nurture our inner ecosystem. When we consistently cater to our emotional, physical, and spiritual needs, we construct a resilient foundation. And upon this foundation, the tower of confidence naturally and effortlessly rises.

Self-care acts as a mirror, reflecting our worth back to us. When we prioritize our well-being, we send a powerful message to our psyche: *"I matter."* This affirmation is the cornerstone of confidence. When we believe we matter, we walk with a sure-footed stride, communicate with conviction, and approach challenges with a can-do attitude.

Moreover, self-care fosters a sense of accomplishment. Each act, whether it's a daily meditation, a commitment to a healthy diet, or setting boundaries in relationships, is a small victory. And these victories accumulate, building a reservoir of self-assuredness. It's similar to a snowball effect; as you take better care of yourself, your confidence grows, and as your confidence grows, you're more inclined to indulge in self-care. It's a virtuous cycle of empowerment!

Now, consider the opposite — a life devoid of self-care. It paints a picture of burnout, fatigue, and self-doubt. When we neglect our needs, we operate from a space of lack, and this deficit is clear in our posture, our voice, and our choices. Without self-care, confidence withers like a plant deprived of sunlight.

To those on the fence about embracing self-care, ponder this: the world perceives you through the lens you offer. When you radiate confidence, borne from genuine self-care, opportunities magnetize towards you. People are drawn to your energy, and the universe itself conspires to uplift you. Your dreams don't just remain figments of imagination; they manifest into reality, all because you had the confidence to chase and achieve them.

Harnessing Confidence Through Self-Care

Self-care is the silent symphony that orchestrates our life's grand performance. It's the magic potion that converts self-doubt into unshakeable confidence. In investing in ourselves, we unlock a world where boundaries blur and potential become limitless. So, embrace self-care and cultivate confidence. And, watch as the world stand in ovation, celebrating the unstoppable force that is you.

In conclusion, self-care is a multifaceted approach to nurturing your physical, mental, emotional, and spiritual well-being. It involves taking deliberate actions to maintain and enhance your health, happiness, and overall quality of life. Here are various types of self-care that encompass different aspects of your being.

Physical Self-Care: The very foundation of our existence! Physical self-care is the art and act of attending to our bodily needs. From the invigorating workouts that sculpt our muscles, to the nourishing foods that fuel us, and the rejuvenating sleep that restores us — this form champions our physiological well-being. Prioritize it, and you're not just surviving; you're thriving with vitality.

Emotional Self-Care: Dive deep into the heart's realm! Emotional self-care is the conscious embrace of our feelings. It's about granting ourselves the grace to feel, to express, and to navigate our emotions. By journaling, seeking therapy, or simply sharing heart-to-heart chats with a confidant, we honor our emotional landscapes, turning tumultuous seas into tranquil waters.

Mental Self-Care: Challenge, stimulate, refresh! Mental self-care recognizes the mind's thirst for growth and rest. Whether you're indulging in enlightening reads, pursuing new hobbies, or taking digital detox breaks, catering to your cognitive well-being ensures you're always sharp, always sparkling.

Social Self-Care: Celebrate connections! Humans are inherently social beings, and this dimension emphasizes the significance of meaningful interactions. Be it heartwarming family dinners, laughter-filled outings with friends, or simply connecting with like-minded communities, nurturing our social bonds invigorates our very spirit.

Spiritual Self-Care: Journey inward and beyond! Regardless of religious beliefs, spiritual self-care is about connecting to something greater than our individual selves. Meditation, prayer, nature walks, or reading spiritual texts—whatever resonates and uplifts your spirit anchors you, granting a profound sense of purpose and peace.

Professional/Career Self-Care: Beyond the 9-to-5 grind! This facet underscores the importance of finding balance and fulfillment in our careers. By setting clear boundaries, taking regular breaks, and pursuing continuous learning, we ensure that our professional lives become sources of pride, not pressure.

Financial Self-Care: Master your money mantra! It's not just about earning and spending, but about fostering a healthy relationship with money. Budgeting, investing, and regular financial check-ins empower you, ensuring you're not just affluent, but also wise and confident in your monetary decisions.

Environmental Self-Care: Embrace your surroundings! This dimension stresses the harmony between us and our environments. By decluttering spaces, choosing sustainable practices, or simply bringing nature indoors with plants, we create sanctuaries that reflect and enhance our inner serenity.

Recreational Self-Care: Revel in recreation! Life isn't all work; there's a playground awaiting your presence. Hobbies, adventures, arts — this form of self-care is all about tapping into activities that light up your soul with sheer joy and passion.

In the vast tapestry of life, these threads of self-care weave together to create a resilient, radiant you. Each dimension, unique yet interconnected, crafts a holistic picture of well-being. Dive into each one. Delve deep. Because when you truly care for yourself, you don't just exist — you exuberantly excel! Dive in, champion self-care, and witness the mesmerizing metamorphosis of your life!

Physical Self-Care Isn't Just Important, It's Essential!

Your body is your ultimate investment. Your physique is your temple, prime real estate. Just as prime property increases in value with care and upkeep, your body's value skyrockets with the right attention. No matter how old you are or what happens in life, you only get one body in this lifetime. It's not available of exchanges or refunds.

We're not talking about merely adding years to your life but life to your years! Dive into a realm where every day feels energized, every moment feels richer, and life's palette is more colorful than ever.

Experience the magic when mind and body harmoniously sync up. Every workout becomes a mood booster, every healthy meal a brain enhancer. Your mental space? Transformed! With a body that's nurtured and fortified, you're not just surviving life's curveballs; you're dominating them!

Physical self-care is the first domino to unlocking unparalleled discipline in all spheres of life. Push that, and witness success in every endeavor cascading before you. Unleash Your Inner Superstar! It's not about the mirror's reflection but the radiating confidence you feel. You won't just walk into a room; you'll own it!

Be Bulletproof! Why wait for health hiccups when you can shield up now? Physical self-care isn't just about feeling good; it's your armor against potential ailments.

Seize the Day – And Your Health!

Harnessing Confidence Through Self-Care

Your body is your most priceless possession. Why not treat it as such? Dive into the realm of physical self-care and witness a world where boundaries blur and potentials are limitless. Start now and shape a legacy of health, vigor, and vitality. After all, you're not just living; you're thriving! There is not a one size fits all approach to physical self-care. It looks different for everyone; the point is to be conscience about proactively maintaining your physical self-care.

On a scale of 1-5, with 5 being the best. How would you rate your physical self-care in the following areas?

_____ Exercise and physical activity

_____ Proper nutrition and a balanced diet

_____ Adequate sleep and rest

_____ Regular medical check-ups

_____ Personal hygiene and grooming

Upon reflecting on your physical self-care quotient, do you feel the need to level up your physical self-care regiment? If so, chart three steps for improvement. If you already exercise great physical self-care, how do you plan to maintain it?

____

____

____

____

____

____

____

What are your physical self-care achievements?

____

____

____

____

____

What are your physical self-care challenges?

____

____

____

____

____

What are your physical self-care adjustments?

____

____

____

____

____

Physical self-care is the art of treasuring your body. It's a silent conversation between you and your well-being, a promise to honor the temple that carries you through life.

Harnessing Confidence Through Self-Care

30-DAY CHALLENGE

NEW HABIT:

Why is this important for me?

Strenghts:

Weaknesses:

Reward:

Let's do this!

How did it go?

What did I learn?

RATE THIS CHALLENGE ☆☆☆☆☆

Reflections

Discover Emotional Self-Care: The Ultimate Elixir for Inner Brilliance!

Your emotions are not just fleeting feelings; they are the illustrious VIP lounge of your heart and soul, a sacred space where your deepest essence thrives. To overlook this emotional realm, it bypasses a chance to experience life in its most vibrant, vivid form. Engaging with your emotions, and you'll discover life in its richest, most colorful intensity.

For many, particularly women, the quest for connections goes beyond surface-level interactions. We yearn for bonds that are not only profound but also genuine and enduring. Herein lies the power of emotional health—it's the golden key unlocking doors to worlds where relationships flourish in the soil of authenticity and mutual respect.

When life unfurls its storms, view them not as obstacles but as canvases for your resilience. With emotional self-care as your compass, you navigate life's challenges not just with grace but with the flair of an artist, transforming trials into triumphs.

Imagine supercharging your mental faculties to their highest potential. That's what emotional wellness offers—a chance to ignite your cognitive prowess, sharpening your thoughts, enhancing your clarity, and brightening your intellect. Emotional self-care is your gateway to a broader, more inclusive worldview. It enables you to bridge cultural divides, comprehend diverse perspectives, and evolve into a true global citizen, embracing and understanding the tapestry of humanity.

In a realm where imitation is rampant, emotional self-care is your pathway to distinctiveness. Delve into the depths of your emotional landscape, unearth your unique essence, and let it radiate with an authenticity that sets you apart.

Liberate yourself from the pursuit of external sources of happiness. Embrace emotional wellness and you tap into a perennial spring of joy, contentment, and enthusiasm for life. This wellspring lies within, a treasure trove of peace and happiness waiting to be unlocked. Emotional self-care is not a mere aspect of your routine—it's a crucial component of your journey towards a fulfilling, authentic, and empowered existence. Prioritize it, nurture it, and watch as your life transforms, mirroring the depth and richness of your emotional well-being.

Dive In, Radiate Out!

Here's the real deal: Emotional self-care isn't an option; it's the main event. It's the shimmering essence that elevates every moment from mundane to magical. Your emotions? They're not just passengers; they're co-pilots on this exhilarating life journey.

So why wait? Embark on the most transformative adventure of your life. Nurture, celebrate, and amplify your emotional landscape. It's not just self-enhancement; it's an upgrade for everything you touch. Because in the world of emotional brilliance, you don't just light up your life; you become the beacon for all. Dive in and dazzle!

On a scale of 1-5, with 5 being the best. How would you rate your emotional self-care in the following areas?

_____ Recognizing and honoring your emotions.

_____ Expressing emotions in a healthy way.

_____ Practicing self-compassion and self-love.

_____ Seeking therapy or counseling when needed.

_____ Creating healthy emotional boundaries.

Upon reflecting on your emotional self-care quotient, do you feel the need to level up your physical self-care regiment? If so, chart three steps for improvement. If you already exercise great physical self-care, how to you plan to maintain it?

____

____

____

____

____

____

____

____

____

____

____

____

What are your emotional self-care achievements?

____

____

____

____

____

What are your emotional self-care challenges?

____

____

____

____

____

What are your emotional self-care adjustments?

____

____

____

____

____

Emotional self-care is the gentle art of listening to your heart, acknowledging your feelings as guides, not adversaries. It's about creating an inner sanctuary of peace, where every emotion is met with compassion and understanding.

Harnessing Confidence Through Self-Care

30-DAY CHALLENGE

NEW HABIT:

Why is this important for me?

Strenghts:

Weaknesses:

Reward:

Let's do this!

How did it go?

What did I learn?

RATE THIS CHALLENGE

Reflections

Unlock the Mind's Magic: The Ultimate Power of Mental Self-Care!

Visualize your mind as the dynamic CEO of 'You, Inc.' – a realm where every decision, breakthrough, and emotion takes root. By elevating the care of your mental landscape, you're not just enhancing an aspect of yourself; you're turbocharging the entirety of your life's experience.

Are you aiming to reach new heights in productivity? Consider mental self-care as your invaluable rocket fuel. Gone are the days of merely chasing dreams. Now, you begin to actualize them with exceptional clarity and sharp focus.

Think of mental self-care as your secret armor of resilience. Challenges and obstacles are part and parcel of life's journey. Yet, with a mind refined and fortified by consistent self-care, you don't just endure these challenges; you rise above them, embracing each with unparalleled zest and determination.

Craving a deluge of innovative thoughts and ideas? A well-nurtured mind becomes the perfect canvas for such creative expression. Prioritize its care and watch as a stream of brilliance and originality flows freely.

When it comes to relationships, it's the quality that triumphs over quantity. A mind steeped in peace and harmony is your passport to forging connections that are not just meaningful but enduring.

Self-evolution is far more than a mere indulgence – it's an essential journey. With mental self-care as your compass, you traverse the path of personal growth and mastery like never before, unlocking levels of self-awareness and achievement that once seemed unattainable.

Let's not forget, the combination of physical vitality, emotional depth, and mental wellness creates a powerful synergy. This triad catalyzes a total transformation, taking you beyond mere wellness into the realm of holistic thriving.

So, here's the essential insight: Your mind is more than just an element of your being; it's the grand orchestrator. Every chapter of adventure, every obstacle surmounted, every triumph celebrated – all are masterfully choreographed in the theater of your mind.

Elevating mental self-care isn't just self-improvement; it's a renaissance of the self. It's the journey of becoming the best version of you, with every thought, every dream, and every action aligned in harmonious symphony. Level up! Delve into the game-changing realm of mental self-care. Gift yourself the clarity of crystal waters, the rejuvenation of a tropical breeze, and the focus of a laser beam. Life's not about watching from the sidelines — it's about orchestrating the grand play.

Illuminate the path of mental wellness as the lifestyle choice. Because when the mind shines, life isn't just good; it's iconic. Join the movement, champion mental vibrancy, and let's craft legendary stories together!

On a scale of 1-5, with 5 being the best. How would you rate your mental self-care in the following areas?

_____ Engaging in stimulating activities for the mind.

_____ Learning and continuous education.

_____ Mindfulness, meditation, and relaxation techniques.

_____ Setting and achieving personal goals.

_____ Challenging and expanding your intellect.

Upon reflecting on your mental self-care quotient, do you feel the need to level up your mental self-care regiment? If so, chart three steps for improvement. If you already exercise great mental self-care, how do you plan to maintain it?

____

____

____

____

____

____

____

____

____

____

____

____

____

What are your mental self-care achievements?

____

____

____

____

____

What are your mental self-care challenges?

____

____

____

____

____

What are your mental self-care adjustments?

____

____

____

____

____

Mental self-care is the quiet revolution within, a journey to the core of your being. It's about cultivating a mind that is both a sanctuary and a powerhouse, where thoughts are not just passing clouds but seeds of potential.

Harnessing Confidence Through Self-Care

30-DAY CHALLENGE

NEW HABIT:

Why is this important for me?

Strenghts:

Weaknesses:

Reward:

Let's do this!

How did it go?

What did I learn?

RATE THIS CHALLENGE ☆☆☆☆☆

Reflections

Amplify Your World: The Non-Negotiable Essence of Social Self-Care!

In the intricate design of the human experience, one detail shines as both fundamental and profound – the need to connect. This isn't a fleeting trend but the pulsating heart of our collective journey. Social self-care is about immersing deeply into this core aspect of our being, allowing our worlds to blossom expansively.

Consider the well-known adage, *it's not what you know, but who you know.* Social self-care reshapes this idea, emphasizing not just who you know, but how you cultivate and cherish these connections. It's about transforming acquaintances into deep, meaningful relationships. Social self-care has the power to elevate our emotional well-being. It turns simple interactions into nourishing experiences, creating bonds that uplift and conversations that heal.

Just as trees require deep roots to reach great heights, our personal development is deeply intertwined with how we foster our social networks, The depth and strength of our connections directly influence the growth and richness of our personal journey.

The art of forming strong, enduring relationships is similar to crafting a legacy. These deep connections aren't stumbled upon; they're deliberately and thoughtfully cultivated. Through prioritizing social self-care, you're not just maintaining friendships; you're building a legacy of lasting relationships that withstand the test of time.

In our vast, diverse, and magnificent world, social self-care is your compass to navigate and appreciate the multitude of cultural nuances. It's about becoming a true global citizen, understanding and embracing the beauty in diversity.

Moreover, social self-care magnifies life's joys. The shared laughter, the collective celebrations - these moments become more vibrant. By investing in your social well-being, every joy is amplified, every triumph shared, making life's journey a richer, more colorful experience.

In sum, social self-care is an essential facet of living a fulfilled life. It's about building bridges, fostering understanding, and celebrating the human connection. Dive into the realm of social self-care, and watch as your life transforms, mirroring the depth and vibrancy of your connections.

Step Into the Social Renaissance!

Here's the golden ticket: Our social fabric isn't a backdrop—it's the main stage. Every laugh, tear, achievement—they're all magnified in the realm of shared experiences.

Ready for a life upgrade? Welcome to the transformative world of social self-care. It's more than mingling—it's art, heart, and smart. Life's not just about individual paths—it's about intersections that create magic. Why blend in when you can stand out? Champion social self-care as the beacon that lights up not just your world but that of others. Because with a vibrant social canvas, life isn't just lived—it's legendary.

Embrace, enrich, and elevate — let's craft social symphonies that resonate for eons!

On a scale of 1-5, with 5 being the best. How would you rate your social self-care in the following areas?

____ Nurturing and maintaining healthy relationships.

____ Establishing boundaries in relationships.

____ Surrounding yourself with positive and supportive people.

____ Spending quality time with loved ones.

____ Joining clubs or communities that align with your interests.

Upon reflecting on your social self-care quotient, do you feel the need to level up your social self-care regiment? If so, chart three steps for improvement. If you already exercise great social self-care, how to you plan to maintain it?

____

____

____

____

____

____

____

____

____

What are your social self-care achievements?

____

____

____

____

____

What are your social self-care challenges?

____

____

____

____

____

What are your social self-care adjustments?

____

____

____

____

____

Social self-care is the art of weaving the fabric of connection, recognizing that our relationships are not just mere encounters but the mirrors of our soul. It's about choosing to surround yourself with those who uplift, inspire, and challenge you in equal measure.

Harnessing Confidence Through Self-Care

30-DAY CHALLENGE

NEW HABIT:

Why is this important for me?

Strenghts:

Weaknesses:

Reward:

Let's do this!

How did it go?

What did I learn?

RATE THIS CHALLENGE ☆☆☆☆☆

Reflections

Elevate Your Essence: The Transformative Power of Spiritual Self-Care!

In the grand narrative of life, where each day expands a myriad of experiences and challenges, there lies a profound dimension often overlooked yet essential for true fulfillment: spiritual self-care. This journey transcends the physical and mental realms, touching the very core of our existence, our spirit.

Spiritual self-care is not confined to religious practices; it's an exploration of the deeper meaning and purpose of our lives. It's about connecting with our innermost self, understanding our place in the universe, and seeking a sense of peace and harmony that resonates beyond the material world. This journey of spiritual self-care is a path of enlightenment, offering clarity in a world often wrapped in chaos. It's about finding tranquility in stillness, wisdom in silence, and strength in introspection. As we embark on this path, we begin to align with our true purpose, our passions, and our values, leading to a life that is not just lived, but deeply experienced.

Spiritual self-care acts as a beacon during times of uncertainty and turmoil. It provides a sense of grounding, a connection to something greater than ourselves, offering solace and perspective when life's storms rage. It encourages us to look beyond the transient and to focus on what truly matters.

Engaging in spiritual self-care cultivates a sense of gratitude and compassion. It opens our hearts to the beauty and interconnectedness of all things and fosters an attitude of mindfulness and appreciation for the present moment.

In essence, spiritual self-care is an integral component of a balanced and fulfilling life. It nourishes the soul, enriches our experiences, and elevates our existence. It's a commitment to nurturing our inner being, to living a life of authenticity, and to finding joy and peace within.

Embark on this sacred journey of spiritual self-care and discover the boundless depths of your soul. In doing so, you'll not only enrich your own life but also bring light and love to those around you.

Embark on the Ultimate Journey!

Here's the revelation: Life isn't merely a physical voyage; it's a profound spiritual odyssey. Every emotion, aspiration, and inspiration—they're all footnotes in this grand spiritual narrative.

Rise to your pinnacle. Step into the realm of spiritual self-care—a world where the ethereal meets the tangible. It's not mere meditation—it's an awakening, an evolution, a rebirth. It's not just about understanding the world—it's about understanding your place in it.

Shatter the mundane. Champion spiritual self-care as your compass to realms unexplored. Because with a soul that's nurtured, life isn't merely a series of events—it's poetry in motion. Soar, transcend, and let's co-create a tapestry that resonates beyond time and space!

Harnessing Confidence Through Self-Care

On a scale of 1-5, with 5 being the best. How would you rate your spiritual self-care in the following areas?

_____ Practicing religion or spirituality that resonates with you.

_____ Meditation, prayer, or mindful reflection.

_____ Connecting with nature and the universe.

_____ Engaging in self-reflection and self-awareness.

_____ Living in alignment with your values and beliefs.

Upon reflecting on your spiritual self-care quotient, do you feel the need to level up your spiritual self-care regiment? If so, chart three steps for improvement. If you already exercise great spiritual self-care, how do you plan to maintain it?

____

____

____

____

____

____

____

____

____

____

____

____

____

What are your spiritual self-care achievements?

____

____

____

____

____

What are your spiritual self-care challenges?

____

____

____

____

____

What are your spiritual self-care adjustments?

____

____

____

____

____

Nurture your spirit, for it is the compass that guides you to your truest path, a beacon of light in the pursuit of inner peace and universal connection.

Harnessing Confidence Through Self-Care

30-DAY CHALLENGE

NEW HABIT:

Why is this important for me?

Strenghts:

Weaknesses:

Reward:

Let's do this!

How did it go?

What did I learn?

RATE THIS CHALLENGE   ☆☆☆☆☆

Reflections

Elevate Your Game: The Unstoppable Force of Professional Self-Care!

When you're navigating your professional journey, where ambition intertwines with achievement, the practice of career self-care emerges not just as a strategy, but as a necessity for crafting a distinguished legacy. It transcends the conventional boundaries of degrees and accolades, guiding you to forge a path that's uniquely yours.

Career self-care is the linchpin in a world enamored with relentless hustle. It's your secret to not merely advancing but advancing with intention, direction, and unyielding purpose. This mindful approach ensures that every step taken is a step toward actualizing your deepest professional aspirations.

Embrace professional challenges with a newfound perspective. Robust career self-care isn't about merely managing tasks; it's about mastering them with exceptional prowess and flair. It's about transforming every challenge into an opportunity to showcase your brilliance.

Networking in the realm of career self-care goes beyond mere exchanges of contact information. It's about cultivating relationships that resonate on a deeper level. Engaging in genuine professional self-care allows your network to expand not just in size but in richness and significance, fostering connections that are both meaningful and impactful.

Consider career self-care as your strategic blueprint for success. It's about setting goals with precision and pursuing them with tenacity. This focused approach ensures that your targets aren't just aspirations but attainable realities.

If you find yourself at a crossroads or stuck in a professional rut, let career self-care be the beacon that guides you back to your path. It's the key to reigniting your passion, rediscovering your purpose, and transitioning from mundane work to a fulfilling career.

In the dynamic and ever-changing landscape of the professional world, adaptability and resilience are invaluable assets. Career self-care equips you with these essential tools, ensuring that you remain not only relevant but also pivotal in your field.

In essence, career self-care is about investing in yourself as a professional. It's about recognizing your potential, valuing your contributions, and continuously evolving. Engage in this practice, and you'll find that you're not just participating in your career; you're shaping it, enjoying it, and excelling in it.

Unveil the Professional Powerhouse Within!

Here's the insider insight: Your professional journey isn't just about external milestones; it's about the internal engine that powers them. Every promotion, project, and proposal — they're all orchestrated by your commitment to professional wellness.

Gear up for supremacy. Embrace the transformative realm of professional self-care — a world where strategy meets soul. It's not just about climbing the ladder — it's about ensuring the ladder is leaning against the right wall.

Break through the glass ceiling, not by brute force, but with finesse. Rally behind professional self-care as your secret sauce to a career that doesn't just pay bills but fulfills dreams. Because with a career crafted with care, you're not just working—you're weaving wonders. Rise, redefine, and let's champion trajectories that inspire generations!

On a scale of 1-5, with 5 being the best. How would you rate your professional self-care in the following areas?

_____ Setting boundaries between work and personal life.

_____ Seeking growth opportunities within your career.

_____ Practicing time management and organization.

_____ Expressing your needs and concerns at the workplace.

_____ Pursuing a fulfilling and meaningful career.

Upon reflecting on your professional self-care quotient, do you feel the need to level up your professional self-care regiment? If so, chart three steps for improvement. If you already exercise great professional self-care, how do you plan to maintain it?

____

____

____

____

____

____

____

____

What are your professional self-care achievements?

____

____

____

____

____

What are your professional self-care challenges?

____

____

____

____

____

What are your professional self-care adjustments?

____

____

____

____

____

Professional self-care is understanding that true success is not measured in achievements, but in the joy and fulfillment found in the journey. It's balancing ambition with well-being, a commitment to excel in your career while honoring your personal boundaries.

Harnessing Confidence Through Self-Care

30-DAY CHALLENGE

NEW HABIT: ____

Why is this important for me? _________________________________

____

Strenghts: ____

Weaknesses: ____

Reward: ____

Let's do this!

How did it go? ____

____

What did I learn? ____

____

RATE THIS CHALLENGE ☆ ☆ ☆ ☆ ☆

Reflections

Master Your Money: The Game-Changing Art of Financial Self-Care!

In the intricate dance of life, where financial stability plays a pivotal role, financial self-care emerges as a cornerstone, not merely for wealth accumulation, but for achieving true freedom. It transcends the traditional view of wealth as a series of numbers, transforming it into a journey towards limitless opportunities and potential.

Financial self-care stands as a lighthouse of empowerment in the unpredictable tides of the economy. It equips you to navigate these waters not just with confidence, but with a sense of mastery and control over your financial destiny. Financial self-care is like a bulletproof shield against the uncertainties of the financial future. It's moving beyond hope as a strategy, stepping into a space where you're fully prepared for any financial scenario that life may present.

This journey is not just about earning money; it's about mastering the art of saving, spending, investing, and making your money work effectively for you. Through the practice of financial self-care, you witness your resources not just grow but flourish, creating a cycle of wealth that continues to expand and enrich your life. Financial self-care transforms your aspirations from distant dreams into achievable destinations. It's about charting a clear course towards financial well-being, navigating each decision with precision and intent, and steadily moving towards a prosperous future.

Financial self-care liberates you from the chains of economic anxiety. It paves the way to a state of inner peace where financial stability is not a sporadic luxury but a consistent, integral part of your life. Finally, consider financial self-care as the foundation for building a legacy. It's about evolving from mere consumption to thoughtful stewardship, ensuring that your financial decisions today pave the way for generational prosperity tomorrow.

In essence, financial self-care is an investment in your future self. It's about taking charge, making informed choices, and paving a path that leads not just to financial security but to a life rich with possibility and peace. Engage in this essential practice, and you'll find that you're not just managing your finances; you're crafting a future replete with prosperity and freedom.

Unlock the Treasury of True Wealth!

Here's the golden truth: Your financial journey isn't just about material wealth—it's about crafting a legacy of lasting prosperity. Every investment, budget, and saving—they're all guided by your commitment to financial wellness.

Step into independence. Welcome to the elite realm of financial self-care—a world where numbers meet nuance. It's not just about financial growth—it's about growth with grace and grit.

Surpass the norm, champion financial self-care as your secret blueprint to a future that doesn't just shimmer with wealth but radiates with rich experiences and security. Because with finances handled with finesse, you're not just living—you're thriving, exponentially. Elevate, enrich, and let's sculpt financial futures that echo with excellence!

On a scale of 1-5, with 5 being the best. How would you rate your financial self-care in the following areas?

____ Budgeting and managing finances effectively.

____ Saving and investing for the future.

____ Being mindful of spending and debt management.

____ Seeking financial advice or education.

____ Planning for financial security and stability.

Upon reflecting on your financial self-care quotient, do you feel the need to level up your financial self-care regiment? If so, chart three steps for improvement. If you already exercise great financial self-care, how to you plan to maintain it?

____

____

____

____

____

____

____

____

____

____

____

____

What are your financial self-care achievements?

____

____

____

____

____

What are your financial self-care challenges?

____

____

____

____

____

What are your financial self-care adjustments?

____

____

____

____

____

Financial self-care is the strategic art of building a future on the foundation of wise choices today. It's about respecting your resources as much as your dreams, understanding that each dollar spent or saved is a vote for the life you wish to lead.

Harnessing Confidence Through Self-Care

30-DAY CHALLENGE

NEW HABIT:

Why is this important for me?

Strenghts:

Weaknesses:

Reward:

Let's do this!

How did it go?

What did I learn?

RATE THIS CHALLENGE ☆☆☆☆☆

Reflections

Embrace Earth Elegance: The Paramount Promise of Environmental Self-Care!

In the grand scheme of existence, your environment is far more than a mere setting; it's the canvas on which the art of your life is painted. Engaging in environmental self-care is a profound journey, transcending mere coexistence to actively coevolving with the natural world around you.

Environmental self-care emerges as a sanctuary of sustainable serenity in our whirlwind lives. It's where tranquility and intent converge, fostering a life lived in beautiful harmony not just within ourselves, but with the universe at large. This practice is an invitation to sync with the planet's rhythm, ensuring that every step we take is in tune with the pulse of the earth.

Consider the elemental necessities of life – clean air, pure water, and untouched landscapes. These are not mere luxuries but the pillars of our well-being. Environmental self-care elevates our health beyond physical boundaries, enveloping our entire being in a cocoon of wellness, nurtured by nature's bounty.

In cultivating environmental self-care, we plant ourselves firmly in the soil of resilience, drawing strength from the enduring vitality of our environment. It's about growing roots that are as deep and enduring as those of the ancient forests, ensuring that we, too, can withstand the test of time and change.

This journey is also a cycle of circular living – a harmonious give and take. It's a commitment to a lifestyle where what we draw from the earth is mindfully replenished. In embracing environmental self-care, we embark on a path of reciprocity, recognizing that every resource borrowed from the earth is a gift to be respected and renewed.

In aligning with our environment, we discover a horizon of holistic happiness. True joy springs from this alignment – found in the simple majesty of a sunrise, the gentle whisper of leaves, and the soothing touch of a dewdrop. It's in these moments that we find a profound balance and contentment.

Environmental wellness is an active choice. It's a commitment to conscious living, making decisions that uplift not only our own lives but also the world around us. Every choice, from the products we use to the footprints we leave, is a stroke on the canvas of our existence, painting a picture that contributes to the health and harmony of our planet.

In essence, environmental self-care is a journey of loving stewardship, a dance of synergy with the earth. It's a path that leads to a life enriched by the planet's beauty and sustained by its wisdom. Engage in this sacred practice and watch as your life transforms into a living testament to the beauty and resilience of the earth.

Forge the Future with Earth Empathy!

Here's the luminous revelation: Your environmental journey isn't just about safeguarding the planet—it's about celebrating its splendor. Every choice, action, and intention— they're all imprints on this grand tapestry of existence.

Step into sustainability. Welcome to the enriching expanse of environmental self-care—a domain where responsibility meets reverence. It's not just about reducing the carbon footprint—it's about leaving footprints of compassion and care. Lead the league. Rally behind environmental self-care as your compass to a world where well-being isn't confined to individuals but extends to the very air we breathe, water we drink, and soil we tread. Because in a world treated with respect and love, life doesn't just sustain—it blossoms, vibrantly and vivaciously. Let's champion a future where care resonates with every echo of the Earth!

On a scale of 1-5, with 5 being the best. How would you rate your environmental self-care in the following areas?

_____ Creating a safe, comfortable, and clean-living space.

_____ Connecting with nature and the outdoors.

_____ Reducing environmental stressors in your surroundings.

_____ Engaging in activities that benefit the environment.

_____ Practicing sustainable living habits.

Upon reflecting on your environmental self-care quotient, do you feel the need to level up your environmental self-care regiment? If so, chart three steps for improvement. If you already exercise great environmental self-care, how do you plan to maintain it?

____

____

____

____

What are your environmental self-care achievements?

____

____

____

____

____

What are your environmental self-care challenges?

____

____

____

____

____

What are your environmental self-care adjustments?

____

____

____

____

____

Environmental self-care is the conscious act of living in harmony with the Earth, recognizing that the care we give to our surroundings reflects the care we give to ourselves.

Harnessing Confidence Through Self-Care

Environmental Self-Care Challenge

30-DAY CHALLENGE

NEW HABIT:

Why is this important for me?

Strenghts:

Weaknesses:

Reward:

Let's do this!

How did it go?

What did I learn?

RATE THIS CHALLENGE ☆☆☆☆☆

Reflections

Unleash Unbridled Joy: The Radiant Realm of Recreational Self-Care!

In this thing we call life, where duties often dominate the score, there is a vital melody that too often goes unsung - the rejuvenating rhythm of recreational self-care. This practice isn't a mere interlude; it's an essential harmony that infuses the soul with vibrant passion and pure delight.

Recreational self-care transcends the traditional notion of merely passing time. It's about intentionally engaging in activities that ignite your spirit, activities that transform leisure into a fuel that powers both heart and mind.

In the relentless marathon that life can be, recreational pauses are not just brief respites. They are potent catalysts for renewed energy and vigor. Embrace these moments, and witness a remarkable ascent in your vitality, a soaring spirit ready to take on life's challenges with newfound enthusiasm.

Imagine a palette where every color represents a possibility, a chance to add vibrancy to the canvas of your existence. Recreational self-care offers just that - a spectrum of experiences that transform the grey hues of routine into a kaleidoscope of exhilarating, enriching moments.

Consider the stresses and strains of daily life. Now, picture the elixir of playful indulgence - the ultimate stressbuster. Engaging in recreational activities is not just escapism; it's a transformative process where tension and worry dissolve into joyous tales and triumphant anecdotes.

But it's not only about the pursuit of fun; it's about embracing freedom. Recreational endeavors broaden your horizons, stretching your skills and reshaping your worldview. They open doors to new perspectives, fostering growth that transcends the physical and permeates every aspect of your being.

Ultimately, recreational self-care is about striking a harmonious balance. It's about finding that sweet spot where work and play not only coexist but synergize, bringing a dynamic, vibrant quality to every facet of life.

Recreational activities, be it a tranquil walk in the woods or a spirited dance to your favorite tune, are far from mere distractions. They are essential nurturers of the spirit, replenishing and revitalizing your essence in the most natural, joyful way.

In essence, recreational self-care is a vital component of a well-rounded, fulfilling life. It's an invitation to live not just efficiently, but exuberantly. Dive into this delightful practice, and experience life not as a series of tasks to be completed, but as a rich tapestry to be savored, celebrated, and cherished.

Ride the Wave of Whimsical Wellness!

Here's the exhilarating essence: Your recreational journey isn't just about leisure—it's about unlocking layers of latent potential and joy. Every game, hobby, and adventure— they're all threads in the vibrant fabric of holistic well-being.

Step into spontaneity. Welcome to the riveting realm of recreational self-care—a space where routine finds rhythm and mundane becomes magical. It's not merely about unwinding— it's about unearthing untapped reservoirs of rapture.

Chart the uncharted. Champion recreational self-care as the key to a life not just lived but relished in resplendent colors. Because in a world where every moment is embraced with enthusiasm and ecstasy, life isn't just fulfilling—it's phenomenally fantastic. Dive, dance, and delight—let's create crescendos of carefree celebration!

On a scale of 1-5, with 5 being the best. How would you rate your recreational self-care in the following areas?

_____ Pursuing hobbies and interests that bring joy.

_____ Taking breaks and vacations to relax and rejuvenate.

_____ Engaging in playful and fun activities.

_____ Attending cultural or artistic events.

_____ Exploring new experiences and adventures.

Upon reflecting on your recreational self-care quotient, do you feel the need to level up your recreational self-care regiment? If so, chart three steps for improvement. If you already exercise great recreational self-care, how do you plan to maintain it?

____

____

____

____

____

____

____

What are your recreational self-care achievements?

____

____

____

____

____

What are your recreational self-care challenges?

____

____

____

____

____

What are your recreational self-care adjustments?

____

____

____

____

____

Embrace recreational self-care, for it is in these moments of uninhibited joy that we rediscover our most authentic selves and recharge our spirits for the journey ahead.

Harnessing Confidence Through Self-Care

30-DAY CHALLENGE

NEW HABIT: ____

Why is this important for me? ___________________________

____

Strenghts: ____

Weaknesses: ____

Reward: ____

Let's do this!

How did it go? ____

____

What did I learn? _____________________________________

____

RATE THIS CHALLENGE ☆☆☆☆☆

Reflections

Remember, self-care is a personalized practice, and what works for one person might not work for another. It's essential to listen to your own needs, preferences, and limitations to create a self-care routine that nurtures and supports your overall well-being.

Your Self-Care Odyssey Begins

Dive deep into any transformative journey, and at its core, you'll discover a guiding force, a blueprint, a north star. When navigating the vast landscape of self-care, this force is manifested in the intentions we set. Intentions are not just goals or resolutions; they're powerful affirmations, heart-felt declarations that illuminate the way, ensuring we move not just with purpose, but with passion.

Setting self-care intentions is like charting a course for a ship. Without it, the vessel, no matter how grand, is at the mercy of the vast sea, susceptible to being lost or going astray. But with clear, defined intentions, the journey becomes not only directed but also enriched with meaning, making every challenge a lesson and every milestone a celebration. So, why is setting self-care intentions paramount?

Clarity in Purpose: In the clamor of external voices and societal expectations, our inner voice—often the truest one—can get drowned out. Setting intentions amplifies this voice, offering clarity. It answers the 'why' behind the 'what', ensuring our actions resonate deeply with our soul's desires.

Focused Energy: Intention acts as a lens, concentrating our energy on what truly matters. It helps filter out distractions, ensuring we invest our time, effort, and emotions in endeavors that truly align with our well-being.

Accountability: An intention is a commitment—a promise we make to ourselves. It becomes a metric, a touchstone, allowing us to assess our journey, celebrating progress, and recalibrating when needed.

Amplified Manifestation: The universe responds to determined will. When we set clear intentions, we send out powerful vibrations, attracting circumstances, opportunities, and energies that align with our aspirations.

Personal Empowerment: At its core, setting self-care intentions is an act of empowerment. It's an assertion that we value ourselves, that we deserve happiness, health, and harmony. It's a declaration that we are not passive spectators but active participants in our life's narrative.

Intentionally set self-care:

- **Reflect Deeply:** *Engage in introspection. Understand where you are and envision where you wish to be.*
- **Be Specific:** *Ambiguous intentions breed scattered results. Be clear, be precise.*
- **Feel the Intention:** *An intention should resonate. Feel its energy, visualize its outcome, savor its fruition in your mind's eye.*
- **Commit to It:** *Write it down, create a vision board, or simply hold it close to your heart. Make it tangible.*
- **Review and Reset:** *Periodically assess. Celebrate milestones and be open to modifying intentions as you evolve.*

Setting self-care intentions isn't just an activity—it's a ritual, an affirmation, a commitment to oneself. In the symphony of life, let your intentions be the notes that create the most harmonious melodies, guiding you towards a radiant, empowered, and fulfilled existence. Start today. Set an intention, even a small one. Feel its power and let it guide you towards unparalleled heights of self-care and self-love.

In today's high-velocity world, where time seems scarce and demands are ever-mounting, we often find ourselves at a crossroads—neglecting the very essence that fuels our journey: our inner self. We have meticulously curated self-care writing prompts, your passport to an internal odyssey of unparalleled depth and discovery.

These prompts are more than mere words—they're a revelation. A beacon guiding you towards the shores of self-awareness, self-love, and a serenity you might've thought elusive. Each question is intricately designed to usher you into spaces of your soul often left unexplored, igniting introspection and birthing clarity. Whether it's forging a deeper connection with your true self, cultivating an environment of tranquility, or simply reigniting the spark of self-love that life's hustle may have dimmed, these prompts stand as your steadfast ally.

But why writing? Because it's raw, real, and remarkably therapeutic. The act of transferring thoughts to paper not only provides clarity but amplifies understanding, making the abstract tangible and the obscure evident. This journey, though personal, promises universal rewards: renewed vigor, heightened self-esteem, and an enriched understanding of one's desires and boundaries.

So, as you stand on the precipice of this enlightening voyage, we invite you to plunge into the depths of these prompts. Navigate the waters of introspection, chart the terrains of self-love, and emerge with a map that leads to your most authentic, vibrant self. Your sanctuary of self-care, a realm where your well-being reigns supreme, is but a pen stroke away. Dive in and discover.

Describe your ideal morning routine that sets a positive tone for the day. How do you prioritize self-care in the morning?

Kickstart your day by listing three things you're grateful for. How does this positive mindset set the tone for your day?

List five things you are grateful for today. How does this practice shape your mindset and overall well-being?

Engage in a session of mindful breathing. Reflect on how it calms your mind and centers your thoughts.

____

____

____

____

____

____

____

____

____

____

____

____

____

____

____

____

____

____

____

____

Celebrate a recent achievement, no matter how small. How did your self-care routine contribute to this success?

____

____

____

____

____

____

____

____

____

____

____

____

____

____

____

____

____

____

____

Detail your ideal 'me-time' activity. How does this rejuvenate your spirit and energize you?

____

____

____

____

____

____

____

____

____

____

____

____

____

____

____

____

____

____

____

Write down three affirmations that boost your confidence and self-worth. How do they influence your mindset throughout the day?

Write down five affirmations related to self-love and repeat
them aloud. How does this practice enhance your self-esteem?

Track your water intake, healthy meals, or exercise for the day.
How do these habits make you feel?

____

____

____

____

____

____

____

____

____

____

____

____

____

____

____

____

____

____

____

____

Harnessing Confidence Through Self-Care

Spend time in nature and describe the experience. How does nature nurture your soul?

Perform a random act of kindness and record it. How does spreading kindness contribute to your well-being?

____

____

____

____

____

____

____

____

____

____

____

____

____

____

____

____

____

____

____

____

Reflect on your day—what went well, what could have been better, and what lessons did you learn for tomorrow?

Record your dreams and feelings upon waking. How do your dreams influence your thoughts and emotions?

Engage in a creative activity—painting, writing, or crafting. How does expressing yourself creatively impact your sense of self?

Declutter a part of your living space. How does a tidier environment contribute to your mental clarity and peace?

Indulge in a sensory experience—light a scented candle, listen to calming music, or enjoy a relaxing bath. How does this soothe your senses?

Practice mindful eating during a meal. How does this enhance your connection with food and its flavors?

Define a personal boundary you want to set. How does this empower you and cultivate self-respect?

Write down something negative you want to release. How does releasing negativity lighten your emotional load?

Outline a step towards achieving a personal goal. How does progressing towards your goals contribute to your overall happiness?

Poised for Power

Dedicate a few hours away from screens. How does a technology detox rejuvenate your mind and senses?

____

____

____

____

____

____

____

____

____

____

____

____

____

____

____

____

____

____

____

Close your eyes and visualize your ideal, peaceful place. How does this mental journey enhance your sense of calm?

Acknowledge and write about three of your unique strengths. How do these strengths empower your daily life?

Describe a challenging situation and how you can approach it with a positive mindset. How does this mental shift impact your outlook?

Write down five affirmations related to self-love and repeat them aloud. How does this practice enhance your self-esteem?

Dedicate an hour to yourself doing something you love. How does this dedicated time rejuvenate your spirit?

Record your stress triggers and coping mechanisms. How does this awareness help you manage stress better?

Harnessing Confidence Through Self-Care

Eat a meal mindfully, paying attention to flavors and textures. How does this mindful approach affect your eating habits?

Write a letter forgiving someone from your past (even if you don't send it). How does releasing resentment lighten your emotional load?

Spend an hour outdoors, absorbing the sights and sounds of nature. How does this natural connection rejuvenate your spirit?

____

____

____

____

____

____

____

____

____

____

____

____

____

____

____

____

____

____

____

Disconnect from technology for an afternoon. How does this break from screens enhance your sense of calm?

____

____

____

____

____

____

____

____

____

____

____

____

____

____

____

____

____

____

____

____

List three things you love about your body. How does practicing body gratitude improve your self-image?

Write a comforting letter to your future self. How does this exercise provide you with reassurance and comfort?

Engage in a creative activity—drawing, writing, or crafting. How does this creative expression nourish your soul?

Create a playlist of songs that will uplift your mood. How does music influence your emotions and mindset?

Practice saying 'no' to a request or commitment that doesn't align with your well-being. How does setting boundaries enhance your self-respect?

Challenge a negative thought and replace it with a positive one.
How does reframing your thoughts boost your self-esteem?

Take a stroll, focusing on all the things you're grateful for in your surroundings. How does this outdoor gratitude practice enrich your perspective?

Write a heartfelt letter to someone you appreciate. How does expressing gratitude strengthen your relationships?

____

____

____

____

____

____

____

____

____

____

____

____

____

____

____

____

____

____

____

____

Organize a part of your living space. How does decluttering your environment contribute to your mental clarity?

Treat yourself to a calming activity like a bath or meditation.
How does this relaxation practice rejuvenate your mind?

List three things that bring you immense joy and plan to do one of them. How does pursuing these joys contribute to your happiness?

Record one positive moment from your day. How does this practice shift your focus towards the good in life?

Perform a random act of kindness and document it. How does spreading kindness enrich your sense of compassion?

Think about a challenge you faced and how you've grown from it. How does recognizing your growth build resilience?

Close your eyes and visualize achieving a dream. How does this visualization exercise motivate you?

Start reading a book you've been eager to explore. How does diving into a good book soothe your mind?

____

____

____

____

____

____

____

____

____

____

____

____

____

____

____

____

____

____

____

Reach out to a friend or family member you haven't spoken to
in a while. How does reconnecting strengthen your bond?

____

____

____

____

____

____

____

____

____

____

____

____

____

____

____

____

____

____

____

Write down your thoughts during a calming evening. How does reflecting at night bring you peace?

Write a short fictional story or poem. How does engaging in creative writing stimulate your imagination?

Celebrate a recent accomplishment, no matter how small. How does recognizing your achievements boost your self-confidence?

____

____

____

____

____

____

____

____

____

____

____

____

____

____

____

____

____

____

____

____

Unveiling Your Soul

At the intersection of authenticity and empowerment lies an invigorating journey — one of self-discovery, unearthing inner strength, and realizing the boundless potential of the soul. This transformative path is often masked under the term we know as 'self-care'. But self-care is not just about moments of relaxation or indulgence; it is a profound act of reclaiming oneself, a strategic endeavor to unleash the brilliance that lies within.

Embarking on the voyage of self-care isn't merely about pampering oneself or indulging in fleeting moments of relaxation. It's a profound journey of introspection, of shedding layers that have perhaps been accumulating over years of neglect, misunderstanding, or self-doubt. It's about digging deep, reaching into the very core of one's being, and embracing what lies therein with love, acceptance, and unwavering confidence.

Each act of self-care is like a brushstroke on a canvas, gradually revealing the masterpiece that is your soul. It starts with the basics – nurturing the body, the vessel that carries the essence of you. Through nutritious meals, mindful exercise, and restful sleep, you begin to glow, radiating an energy that's palpable. This physical transformation, though significant, is just the beginning.

With a rejuvenated body, the mind becomes receptive, ready to be molded and strengthened. Meditation, journaling, affirmations - these become tools in the arsenal of the awakened. They chisel away at insecurities, replacing them with a rock-solid foundation of self-belief. As the fog of self-doubt lifts, a clarity emerges. The understanding that you are not just a product of your past or a puppet of your circumstances. You are the master of your fate, the captain of your soul. This realization is the true essence of confidence.

But the journey doesn't end there. With a fortified mind and body, the spirit seeks nourishment. This is where deeper practices of self-care come into play. Engaging in soulful conversations, seeking purpose, aligning with passions, and forging connections that uplift - these acts unveil the ethereal, the divine within.

Now, some may question the link between self-care and confidence. To them, we say, "Witness the transformation of the caterpillar." It's through nurturing itself, honoring its process, and surrendering to its journey that it emerges as a butterfly. Self-care is the cocoon. And when practiced with intent, consistency, and reverence, one emerges with wings of confidence, ready to soar.

In essence, self-care is not a luxury; it's a necessity. It's the key to unlocking potential, to transcending limits, to realizing dreams. In a world that often demands conformity, where the cacophony of others' expectations can drown out the whispers of one's heart, self-care becomes the sanctuary. It's the sacred space where you meet yourself, without judgments, without masks.

Harnessing Confidence Through Self-Care

As you unveil each layer, as you discover each facet, there's a realization of the boundless possibilities that lie within. Confidence is not about knowing you'll succeed; it's about trusting yourself regardless of the outcome. And that trust is cultivated when you truly, deeply, and completely care for yourself.

So, dare to dive deep. Commit to the ritual of self-renewal, of soulful unveiling. Let self-care be the wind beneath your wings, propelling you towards horizons unknown, adventures untold, and a version of you that's been waiting, with bated breath, to confidently shine.

Crafting Your Serene Journey

In the sprawling canvas of existence, where chaos often reigns and tumultuous tides rise, there's a journey waiting to be embarked upon—a serene odyssey. An adventure not of external landscapes, but of inner sanctuaries. An exploration so profound that its trails lead to the very heart of tranquility and peace.

Imagine, if you will, your life as a masterfully crafted ship. While external storms may batter and challenges loom like treacherous rocks, within the vessel lies a calm, still oasis, untouched by the world's turbulence. This serene odyssey is the voyage to discover and cultivate that sanctuary.

Why, in life's unending hustle, is there a need to seek this serenity? Because in serenity lies power. The power to think clearly, to act with purpose, and to live with intention. In the hushed whispers of calm, we hear the loudest truths. It's the pause between heartbeats, the silence between notes, that crafts the most beautiful symphonies of life.

Crafting your serene odyssey requires a blend of courage and vulnerability. It's a journey of introspection. Begin by setting sail on the sea of self-awareness. Recognize the patterns, the anchors, the winds that propel your ship. What are the passions that set your soul aflame? What are the fears that cast shadows on your deck? By understanding these, you craft the map for your journey.

Equip your vessel with tools of mindfulness. Let meditation be your compass, guiding you through the misty realms of the mind. Let gratitude be your anchor, grounding you amidst life's high tides. And let self-love be your guiding star, illuminating even the darkest of nights.

But crafting this odyssey is not an act of isolation. It's about forging connections too—connections that enrich and elevate. Surround yourself with souls who reflect your light, who resonate with your quest. Share stories, exchange wisdom, and build a fellowship of serenity seekers.

And then, there's the art of letting go. Every serene odyssey demands a release of excess baggage. The regrets of the past, the anxieties of the future—they only weigh your vessel down. Release them. Allow the currents of forgiveness and acceptance to carry them away, leaving behind only clarity and peace.

However, remember this: the serene odyssey is not a destination but a continuous voyage. Just as the sea changes its hues and moods, so will the landscapes of your inner world. The key is to stay adaptable, to dance with the ebb and flow, to find beauty in both the still waters and the stormy waves. In crafting this journey, you're not merely seeking serenity; you're becoming it. You're transforming into a beacon of calm, radiating tranquility to every soul that crosses your path. Your very presence becomes a sanctuary, a testament to the wonders of inner peace.

In conclusion, within the disharmony of life's orchestra, there exists a melody—a serene, harmonious tune that sings of inner peace and balance. Crafting your serene odyssey is about tuning into this melody, about becoming one with it. So, chart your course, captain your ship, and sail into the uncharted waters of the soul. Discover the treasures of tranquility that lie deep within, embrace them, and let them guide your way. Because when you embark on your serene odyssey, you don't just navigate life — you transcend it. Dive deep, embrace the calm, and watch as the world stands in awe of the serene saga that unfolds!

Serenity Score Card

The Serenity Scorecard is a reflective tool designed to help you gauge your current state of peace, balance, and contentment in various aspects of your life. By understanding where you stand, you can work towards enhancing your well-being. Use this scorecard monthly or whenever you feel the need to check in with yourself.

Instructions: On a scale of 1 to 10 (with 1 being Not at all and 10 being Completely), rate each statement based on how true it feels for you currently.

Physical Serenity:

I feel physically relaxed and free from tension. ___/10

My sleep patterns are regular, and I wake up feeling refreshed. ___/10

My dietary choices make me feel nourished and energized. ___/10

I engage in regular physical activities that I enjoy. ___/10

My physical surroundings (home, workspace) are clutter-free and bring me peace. ___/10

Emotional Serenity:

I feel emotionally balanced and stable most of the time. ___/10

I have effective strategies to cope with stress and negative emotions. ___/10

I regularly experience feelings of gratitude and contentment. ___/10

I feel connected and understood in my relationships. ___/10

I allow myself to experience and express a wide range of emotions. ___/10

Mental Serenity:

I have clarity about my goals and priorities. ___/10

I regularly engage in activities that challenge and stimulate my mind. ___/10

I feel confident in my decision-making abilities. ___/10

I avoid overcommitting and know how to set boundaries. ___/10

I take breaks to clear my mind when I feel overwhelmed. ___/10

Spiritual Serenity:

I feel a deep sense of purpose and meaning in my life. ___/10

I engage in spiritual or meditative practices that enrich my soul. ___/10

I feel connected to something larger than myself. ___/10

I regularly spend time in nature or in environments that uplift my spirit. ___/10

I am accepting and non-judgmental towards myself and others. ___/10

Total Score: ___/200

Interpreting Your Score:

160 - 200: You're thriving! You have a strong foundation of serenity in your life. Keep up the practices that are working for you.

120 - 159: You're on the right path. There may be specific areas to focus on, but you're cultivating a good sense of balance.

80 - 119: Consider this a nudge to pay more attention to your well-being. Reflect on areas of low scores to determine actions.

Below 80: It might be helpful to seek support. Remember, it's okay to ask for help, whether it's from friends, family, or professionals.

Remember, this scorecard is a tool for reflection, not a definitive measure. Your feelings and experiences are valid regardless of the score. Adjustments and self-care are ongoing journeys. Keep revisiting and recalibrating to ensure you're moving towards the serenity you deserve.

Imagine the most tranquil, fulfilling moments of your life. What are the common elements and significance in these memories?

Think of challenges that have disrupted your serenity in the past. How did you navigate them?

Write a persuasive guide for your future self, detailing strategies to gracefully sail through life's stormy seas, ensuring that the journey remains serene even when the waters are rough.

Reflect on the individuals who amplify your sense of peace and those who might challenge it. Why do these individuals have such an impact on your journey?

Envision the rewards reaped from a life lived in serene harmony. How do these treasures manifest in your health, relationships, and overall well-being?

____

____

____

____

____

____

____

____

____

____

____

____

____

____

____

____

____

____

____

____

Design a day infused with rituals and habits that anchor you in tranquility. Detail each ritual, from a morning meditation to an evening gratitude journal.

____

____

____

____

____

____

____

____

____

____

____

____

____

____

____

____

____

____

____

____

Radiate with Self-Love

In the vast galaxy of existence, where stars shimmer and planets parade, there exists an energy so potent, so transformative, that it has the power to outshine even the sun. This luminous force? The radiant glow of self-love.

Picture it: the heart's core, ablaze with an indomitable flame, powered by an unwavering love for oneself. Self-love isn't just a concept—it's an art, a lifestyle, a revolution. It's the conscious decision to stand before the mirror of life, gazing deeply, and declaring, "I am enough. I am worthy. I am spectacular."

But why, in a world bursting with distractions, must we champion self-love with such fervor? Because self-love is the foundation upon which we construct our universe. It's the compass that guides our choices, the shield that defends against doubts, and the elixir that heals wounds both old and new. When we love ourselves—truly, deeply, passionately— we become invincible. We become the architects of our destiny, crafting realities that shimmer with promise and joy.

With self-love, every nook and cranny of our being radiates confidence. Imagine stepping into a room, and without uttering a word, your very presence speaks volumes. The way you carry yourself, the gleam in your eyes, the unapologetic authenticity—it's magnetic. People are drawn not just to your outward charm, but to the incredible love story unfolding within you, the one where you're both the lover and the beloved.

Embracing self-love also means recognizing and celebrating our imperfections. It's about understanding that we are masterpieces, with each flaw adding depth and character to our story. In a society that often promotes unattainable standards, self-love rebels. It whispers, "You are perfect in your imperfections, splendid in your uniqueness."

Moreover, self-love acts as the catalyst for external love. When we adore our essence, we radiate positivity, attracting relationships that mirror this affection. Our interactions bloom with genuine warmth and mutual respect. We no longer seek validation; instead, we become the source of affirmation, not just for ourselves, but for everyone we encounter.

And then there's the magic of manifestation. Rooted in self-love, our aspirations soar. We believe in our dreams and, more importantly, in our capability to realize them. Every challenge becomes an exciting puzzle, every setback a plot twist. With self-love as our anchor, we navigate life's storms with grace and tenacity.

So, how does one embark on this radiant journey? Begin by tuning into your inner dialogue. Shower yourself with words of encouragement, compassion, and admiration. Celebrate your victories, however small. Cultivate rituals that nourish your soul: meditate, journal, dance, sing! Surround yourself with energies that uplift and inspire. But above all, commit to this love affair with yourself. Promise to stand by your side, come what may.

In conclusion, self-love is the symphony that orchestrates our existence. It's the song of the soul, the dance of the spirit. As you stand at the crossroads of life, make the choice to journey inward. Discover the treasures that lie within, embrace them, and let them shine. Because when you radiate self-love, you don't just light up your world—you illuminate the universe. Dive into this love odyssey and watch as the world marvels at the dazzling star that is YOU!

Imagine standing before a mirror that doesn't reflect your physical appearance but showcases your unique qualities. What colors, symbols, and words appear? Persuade yourself to recognize and embrace these intrinsic values every day.

Recall a moment in your life when you felt a lack of self-love. How would radiating self-love have changed your reactions, decisions, and the outcome?

Pen a heartfelt letter to your younger self. Fill it with words of encouragement, lessons you've learned about self-worth, and assurances of the magnificent journey ahead.

____

____

____

____

____

____

____

____

____

____

____

____

____

____

____

____

____

____

____

____

Visualize a world where every decision you make is guided by profound self-love. How would your daily routines, relationships, and aspirations evolve?

Design a virtual gallery filled with affirmations that resonate with your journey of self-love. Why are these affirmations pivotal in ensuring you continually radiate self-love?

The Art of Prioritizing You

Amid the bustling symphony of life, where countless roles demand your performance, where myriad voices seek your attention, there lies a melody often overlooked. It's the harmonious tune of self, the rhythm of prioritizing YOU. This is not merely an act—it's an art. An art as exquisite as sculpting a masterpiece, as intricate as penning an epic. The masterpiece and epic, in this case, being the radiant and full life, you deserve.

The world is brimming with commitments. From the urgent buzz of work notifications to the soft tug of familial expectations, the demands seem endless. Yet, in this vast expanse of responsibilities, where does one's responsibility to oneself fit in? Here's the persuasive truth: amidst these swirling obligations, the most crucial commitment is the one you make to yourself.

Now, "Prioritizing You" is not a call to dismiss external duties or shun worldly engagements. Instead, it's a compelling invitation to place oneself on the priority list—high up, glowing, unapologetic. For when you fill your cup first, you overflow with abundance, grace, and vitality, enriching everything and everyone you touch.

But how does one master this art? The canvas of self-value awaits, and here's how you paint it vibrantly:

Awareness: Recognize your worth. It's not vanity—it's clarity. Understand that you, with your dreams, desires, and well-being, matter immensely. This acknowledgment is the first brushstroke.

Boundaries: Sculpt your space. Just as an artist wouldn't let anyone smudge their creation, don't let the world blur your boundaries. Set them firmly, lovingly, ensuring that they protect your peace and passion.

Self-Reflection: Dive into the introspective pool. Understand what invigorates you, what drains you. Tailor your day, your life around these insights. Craft a routine that celebrates you.

Self-Nurturing: Indulge in activities that rejuvenate your spirit. Whether it's reading a book, meditating, or simply sipping tea while watching the sunrise, these moments are not luxuries—they're essentials. They're the vibrant hues on your canvas.

Affirmations: Talk to yourself, and let it be a conversation of love, respect, and encouragement. Your inner dialogue should be the most empowering voice you hear.

Seek Growth: Embrace opportunities that amplify your potential. Prioritizing you is not just about relaxation—it's about evolution. Invest in skills, experiences, and knowledge that magnify your essence.

Here's the thing: the world will always have expectations. Tasks will multiply, calendars will overflow. But in the midst of this chaos, the sanctuary of self-prioritization stands tall. By honoring this sanctuary, you're not diminishing other aspects of life; you're enhancing them. For a nurtured, valued, prioritized self can contribute to the world with unparalleled vigor and joy.

In conclusion, the art of prioritizing you is a journey—a journey to the heart of self-value. It's a commitment to ensuring that in the theater of life, the leading role, filled with zest and brilliance, is played by YOU. So, embrace this art, refine it, and let it elevate your existence. For when you prioritize yourself, you don't just live—you thrive, you shine, you create magic. Step into this spotlight, wear your crown of self-worth, and watch as the world applauds the magnificent saga of YOU.

Envision a world where you consistently prioritize your needs, passions, and well-being. How would this renewed commitment to yourself impact the world around you?

____

____

____

____

____

____

____

____

____

____

____

____

____

____

____

____

____

____

Harnessing Confidence Through Self-Care

List areas in your life where boundaries are blurry or non-existent. What steps can you take to redefine and solidify these boundaries? Why are these changes essential for your growth and happiness?

Recall three recent instances where you said "yes" when your heart truly wanted to say "no." Why is it crucial for you to harness the power of "no" more often?

Describe your ideal day of self-care and personal indulgence. How does this day make you feel, and why is it essential to carve out such moments regularly?

____

____

____

____

____

____

____

____

____

____

____

____

____

____

____

____

____

____

____

____

Write a persuasive letter from this future self to your present self, detailing the joys, accomplishments, and peace this path brought and urging you to remain steadfast in this commitment.

____

____

____

____

____

____

____

____

____

____

____

____

____

____

____

____

____

____

____

Your Ultimate Self-Care Checklist

Physical Wellness

- ✓ Regular Exercise: Commit to a routine that energizes your body.
- ✓ Balanced Nutrition: Fuel your body with a variety of healthy foods.
- ✓ Adequate Sleep: Prioritize restful sleep to rejuvenate your body and mind.
- ✓ Hydration: Keep your body hydrated for optimal health.
- ✓ Routine Check-ups: Stay on top of your health with regular medical screenings.

Emotional Balance

- ✓ Mindfulness Practice: Engage in daily meditation or deep-breathing exercises.
- ✓ Express Feelings: Regularly share your emotions through journaling or conversations.
- ✓ Stress Management: Identify stressors and develop coping mechanisms.
- ✓ Quality Time Alone: Reserve moments for self-reflection and solitude.
- ✓ Joyful Activities: Do things that make you happy and bring you peace.

Mental Fortitude

- ✓ Learning and Growth: Dedicate time to learning new skills or hobbies.
- ✓ Positive Affirmations: Start your day with empowering and positive thoughts.

- ✓ Mental Breaks: Take short breaks throughout the day to clear your mind.
- ✓ Limit Screen Time: Reduce exposure to digital screens, especially before bedtime.
- ✓ Seek Inspiration: Read, listen to podcasts, or watch content that uplifts you.

Spiritual Connection

- ✓ Nature Time: Spend time outdoors to connect with nature.
- ✓ Spiritual Practices: Engage in activities that nourish your spirit, like yoga or meditation.
- ✓ Gratitude: Maintain a daily gratitude practice.
- ✓ Community Involvement: Participate in community or volunteer work.
- ✓ Reflection: Spend time in introspection to align with your values and beliefs.

Social Fulfillment

- ✓ Connect with Loved Ones: Regularly communicate with friends and family.
- ✓ Networking: Engage in meaningful conversations with new people.
- ✓ Support System: Build and maintain a supportive network.
- ✓ Boundary Setting: Clearly communicate and maintain your personal boundaries.
- ✓ Collaborative Activities: Participate in group activities that bring joy and collaboration.

Professional Enrichment

- ✓ Skill Enhancement: Continuously work on improving your professional skills.
- ✓ Work-Life Balance: Strive for a balance that respects your personal life.
- ✓ Positive Work Environment: Cultivate a workspace that inspires productivity and positivity.
- ✓ Career Goals: Set and review short-term and long-term professional goals.
- ✓ Recognition: Acknowledge and celebrate your professional achievements.

Financial Health

- ✓ Budgeting: Regularly monitor and plan your finances.
- ✓ Savings: Set aside a portion of income for savings.
- ✓ Investing in Self: Allocate resources for personal development and health.
- ✓ Financial Literacy: Continuously educate yourself about financial management.
- ✓ Debt Management: Strategically plan and reduce debts.

This checklist is more than a to-do list; it's your roadmap to a holistic, balanced, and fulfilling life. Check off these items not as chores, but as steppingstones to a happier, healthier you. Remember, self-care is a personal journey, unique to each individual. Tailor these steps to fit your lifestyle and watch as you flourish in all aspects of your life.

Create Your Own Self-Care Checklist

❑ ____

❑ ____

❑ ____

❑ ____

❑ ____

❑ ____

❑ ____

❑ ____

❑ ____

❑ ____

❑ ____

❑ ____

❑ ____

❑ ____

❑ ____

❑ ____

❑ ____

❑ ____

Harnessing Confidence Through Self-Care

Your Journey's Epilogue

As the pages of this self-care journal come to a close, let's pause for a moment, basking in the radiance of your journey — a journey that has been as transformative as it has been enlightening. This wasn't merely a collection of pages, prompts, and penned thoughts, it was an intimate rendezvous with your deepest self, a dialogue with your innermost aspirations and desires, an exploration into the sanctum of your soul.

Each word you've scribed within these pages is a testament to your commitment — to grow, to heal, to love, and most importantly, to prioritize yourself and well-being. With every entry, you've unraveled layers, confronted fears, and celebrated victories, no matter how minute. Through introspective inquiries and contemplative exercises, you've delicately woven the tapestry of your serene journey, colorfully adorned with moments of epiphany and clarity.

The magic of this journal lies in your responses. It's the raw emotion, the candid revelations, and the vulnerable truths that have painted a vivid portrait of who you are and who you aspire to be. This journal has been the mirror reflecting your strengths, illuminating areas for growth, and most crucially, reminding you of your immeasurable worth.

While this journal may be concluding, your journey is far from over. Think of this experience as a steppingstone, an empowering foundation upon which you can build towering edifices of self-awareness, self-love, and holistic well-being. The insights gleaned and the wisdom acquired are tools — tools that empower you to navigate the vast oceans of life with a compass calibrated by genuine self-care.

So, what's next? First, regularly revisit these pages. They're not just a record but a living testament of your evolution. Reflect on your insights, marvel at your growth, and recognize areas that might beckon further exploration. Second, be the ambassador of self-care. Share your revelations, inspire others, and let your journey illuminate the path for many.

But above all, remain committed. Self-care isn't a destination; it's a continuous journey. A voyage that demands regular introspection, consistent efforts, and an undying commitment to oneself. As days turn into weeks and weeks into months, challenges will arise, and waves of doubt might attempt to deter you. But remember this: the sanctuary of self-care you've cultivated within these pages is your anchor. It's your sanctuary during storms, your North Star amidst uncertainties.

In closing, extend gratitude to yourself for embarking on this remarkable endeavor. You've shown up for yourself, day in and day out, and that's a victory in itself. This self-care guided journal was but a vessel; the true navigator, the real hero of this story, has always been you. Here's to the next chapter, to continuing the journey, and to always prioritizing the art of self-care. Cheers to you, the radiant soul, the fierce warrior, the ever-evolving masterpiece.

Your Roadmap to a Transformative Self-Care Regimen

Embarking on a self-care journey is akin to charting a course for uncharted waters. It requires intent, dedication, and a compass of self-awareness. Here's your expertly crafted roadmap to guide you through establishing and flourishing in your self-care regimen:

1. Self-Assessment: Define Your Needs

- ***Reflect and Recognize:*** *Start by taking stock of your current state. What areas of your life need more attention? Physical health, emotional well-being, mental clarity, spiritual growth?*
- ***Set Clear Objectives:*** *Define what success looks like for you in each area. Is it more energy, better stress management, deeper connections?*

2. Design Your Custom Self-Care Plan

- ***Tailored Actions:*** *Based on your assessment, curate activities for each aspect of self-care. For physical health, it might be yoga or jogging; for mental wellness, perhaps meditation or reading.*
- ***Balanced Approach:*** *Ensure your plan is holistic – covering physical, mental, emotional, and spiritual self-care.*

3. Schedule and Routine Building

- ***Integrate into Daily Life:*** *Pencil your self-care activities into your daily routine. Make them as non-negotiable as a business meeting.*
- ***Gradual Progression:*** *Start small and gradually increase the intensity or duration of your activities. Consistency is key.*

4. Establish Support Systems

- ***Seek Accountability:*** *Share your journey with a friend, join a group, or consider a coach for accountability.*
- ***Gather Resources:*** *Equip yourself with necessary tools – be it a yoga mat, a journal, meditation apps, or educational materials.*

5. Monitor and Reflect

- ***Regular Check-ins:*** *Schedule weekly or monthly check-ins with yourself. Are you sticking to your plan? How do you feel physically, mentally, emotionally?*
- ***Journal Your Journey:*** *Keep a record of your progress and setbacks. This is crucial for self-awareness and motivation.*

6. Adapt and Evolve

- ***Be Flexible:*** *If something isn't working, be open to adjusting your approach. Self-care is personal and should evolve with you.*
- ***Stay Informed:*** *Keep abreast of new self-care trends, research, and techniques. Continuous learning is part of the journey.*

7. Celebrate Milestones

- *Acknowledge Progress:* Celebrate your victories, no matter how small. Did you meditate for ten days straight? Reward yourself!
- *Reflect on Growth:* Regularly look back on how far you've come. It's about progress, not perfection.

8. Cultivate a Self-Care Mindset

- *Positive Affirmations:* Use positive affirmations to reinforce your commitment to self-care.
- *Patience and Compassion:* Be patient with yourself. Change takes time, and self-care is a lifelong journey.

9. Share and Inspire

- *Be a Role Model:* As you progress, share your story with others. Your journey can inspire someone to embark on their own.
- *Community Engagement:* Join or form communities that focus on self-care. There's power in shared experiences.

In summary, your journey to a robust self-care regimen is not just a path to better health and happiness; it's a commitment to your most important asset – you. Follow this roadmap with conviction and watch as you unfold into the best version of yourself, equipped with resilience, vitality, and a profound sense of well-being. Onward to a transformative journey of self-care!

Reflections

GOALS TODAY

What are your top goals to accomplish for the day?

TO-DO LIST

Check off your tasks throughout the day.

FREE THOUGHTS

TODAY I'M GRATEFUL FOR

what makes you feel blessed for the day?

-
-
-

SOMETHING THAT INSPIRES ME

what sparks your creativity today?

-
-
-

TODAY'S AFFIRMATIONS

words to define your day

-
-
-

MY SELF-CARE INCLUDED:

Harnessing Confidence Through Self-Care

GOALS TODAY
What are your top goals to accomplish for the day?

TO-DO LIST
Check off your tasks throughout the day.

FREE THOUGHTS

TODAY I'M GRATEFUL FOR

what makes you feel blessed for the day?

-
-
-

SOMETHING THAT INSPIRES ME

what sparks your creativity today?

-
-
-

TODAY'S AFFIRMATIONS

words to define your day

-
-
-

MY SELF-CARE INCLUDED:

Harnessing Confidence Through Self-Care

DATE   /   /

GOALS TODAY
What are your top goals to accomplish for the day?

TO-DO LIST
Check off your tasks throughout the day.

FREE THOUGHTS

TODAY I'M GRATEFUL FOR

what makes you feel blessed for the day?

-
-
-

SOMETHING THAT INSPIRES ME

what sparks your creativity today?

-
-
-

TODAY'S AFFIRMATIONS

words to define your day

-
-
-

MY SELF-CARE INCLUDED:

Harnessing Confidence Through Self-Care

GOALS TODAY
What are your top goals to accomplish for the day?

TO-DO LIST
Check off your tasks throughout the day.

FREE THOUGHTS

TODAY I'M GRATEFUL FOR

what makes you feel blessed for the day?

-
-
-

SOMETHING THAT INSPIRES ME

what sparks your creativity today?

-
-
-

TODAY'S AFFIRMATIONS

words to define your day

-
-
-

MY SELF-CARE INCLUDED:

Harnessing Confidence Through Self-Care

GOALS TODAY
What are your top goals to accomplish for the day?

TO-DO LIST
Check off your tasks throughout the day.

FREE THOUGHTS

TODAY I'M GRATEFUL FOR

what makes you feel blessed for the day?

-
-
-

SOMETHING THAT INSPIRES ME

what sparks your creativity today?

-
-
-

TODAY'S AFFIRMATIONS

words to define your day

-
-
-

MY SELF-CARE INCLUDED:

Harnessing Confidence Through Self-Care

GOALS TODAY
What are your top goals to accomplish for the day?

TO-DO LIST
Check off your tasks throughout the day.

FREE THOUGHTS

Poised for Power

TODAY I'M GRATEFUL FOR

what makes you feel blessed for the day?

-
-
-

SOMETHING THAT INSPIRES ME

what sparks your creativity today?

-
-
-

TODAY'S AFFIRMATIONS

words to define your day

-
-
-

MY SELF-CARE INCLUDED:

GOALS TODAY

What are your top goals to accomplish for the day?

TO-DO LIST

Check off your tasks throughout the day.

FREE THOUGHTS

TODAY I'M GRATEFUL FOR

what makes you feel blessed for the day?

-
-
-

SOMETHING THAT INSPIRES ME

what sparks your creativity today?

-
-
-

TODAY'S AFFIRMATIONS

words to define your day

-
-
-

MY SELF-CARE INCLUDED:

Harnessing Confidence Through Self-Care

DATE   /   /

GOALS TODAY
What are your top goals to accomplish for the day?

TO-DO LIST
Check off your tasks throughout the day.

FREE THOUGHTS

Poised for Power

TODAY I'M GRATEFUL FOR

what makes you feel blessed for the day?

-
-
-

SOMETHING THAT INSPIRES ME

what sparks your creativity today?

-
-
-

TODAY'S AFFIRMATIONS

words to define your day

-
-
-

MY SELF-CARE INCLUDED:

Harnessing Confidence Through Self-Care

GOALS TODAY
What are your top goals to accomplish for the day?

TO-DO LIST
Check off your tasks throughout the day.

FREE THOUGHTS

Poised for Power

TODAY I'M GRATEFUL FOR

what makes you feel blessed for the day?

-
-
-

SOMETHING THAT INSPIRES ME

what sparks your creativity today?

-
-
-

TODAY'S AFFIRMATIONS

words to define your day

-
-
-

MY SELF-CARE INCLUDED:

Harnessing Confidence Through Self-Care

DATE   /   /

GOALS TODAY
What are your top goals to accomplish for the day?

TO-DO LIST
Check off your tasks throughout the day.

FREE THOUGHTS

TODAY I'M GRATEFUL FOR

what makes you feel blessed for the day?

-
-
-

SOMETHING THAT INSPIRES ME

what sparks your creativity today?

-
-
-

TODAY'S AFFIRMATIONS

words to define your day

-
-
-

MY SELF-CARE INCLUDED:

GOALS TODAY
What are your top goals to accomplish for the day?

TO-DO LIST
Check off your tasks throughout the day.

FREE THOUGHTS

DATE   /   /

TODAY I'M GRATEFUL FOR

what makes you feel blessed for the day?

-
-
-

SOMETHING THAT INSPIRES ME

what sparks your creativity today?

-
-
-

TODAY'S AFFIRMATIONS

words to define your day

-
-
-

MY SELF-CARE INCLUDED:

Harnessing Confidence Through Self-Care

GOALS TODAY

What are your top goals to accomplish for the day?

TO-DO LIST

Check off your tasks throughout the day.

FREE THOUGHTS

DATE / /

TODAY I'M GRATEFUL FOR

what makes you feel blessed for the day?

-
-
-

SOMETHING THAT INSPIRES ME

what sparks your creativity today?

-
-
-

TODAY'S AFFIRMATIONS

words to define your day

-
-
-

MY SELF-CARE INCLUDED:

Harnessing Confidence Through Self-Care

GOALS TODAY

What are your top goals to accomplish for the day?

TO-DO LIST

Check off your tasks throughout the day.

FREE THOUGHTS

TODAY I'M GRATEFUL FOR

what makes you feel blessed for the day?

-
-
-

SOMETHING THAT INSPIRES ME

what sparks your creativity today?

-
-
-

TODAY'S AFFIRMATIONS

words to define your day

-
-
-

MY SELF-CARE INCLUDED:

Harnessing Confidence Through Self-Care

GOALS TODAY

What are your top goals to accomplish for the day?

TO-DO LIST

Check off your tasks throughout the day.

FREE THOUGHTS

TODAY I'M GRATEFUL FOR

what makes you feel blessed for the day?

-
-
-

SOMETHING THAT INSPIRES ME

what sparks your creativity today?

-
-
-

TODAY'S AFFIRMATIONS

words to define your day

-
-
-

MY SELF-CARE INCLUDED:

Harnessing Confidence Through Self-Care

GOALS TODAY
What are your top goals to accomplish for the day?

TO-DO LIST
Check off your tasks throughout the day.

FREE THOUGHTS

TODAY I'M GRATEFUL FOR

what makes you feel blessed for the day?

-
-
-

SOMETHING THAT INSPIRES ME

what sparks your creativity today?

-
-
-

TODAY'S AFFIRMATIONS

words to define your day

-
-
-

MY SELF-CARE INCLUDED:

Harnessing Confidence Through Self-Care

DATE   / /   **DAILY GOALS**

GOALS TODAY
What are your top goals to accomplish for the day?

TO-DO LIST
Check off your tasks throughout the day.

FREE THOUGHTS

Poised for Power

TODAY I'M GRATEFUL FOR

what makes you feel blessed for the day?

-
-
-

SOMETHING THAT INSPIRES ME

what sparks your creativity today?

-
-
-

TODAY'S AFFIRMATIONS

words to define your day

-
-
-

MY SELF-CARE INCLUDED:

Harnessing Confidence Through Self-Care

GOALS TODAY

What are your top goals to accomplish for the day?

TO-DO LIST

Check off your tasks throughout the day.

FREE THOUGHTS

DATE   /   /   **DAILY EVALUATION**

TODAY I'M GRATEFUL FOR

what makes you feel blessed for the day?

-
-
-

SOMETHING THAT INSPIRES ME

what sparks your creativity today?

-
-
-

TODAY'S AFFIRMATIONS

words to define your day

-
-
-

MY SELF-CARE INCLUDED:

Harnessing Confidence Through Self-Care

Reflections

Reflections

Reflections

Reflections

Poised for Power

Discover the essence of empowerment with MeEvolv Devotionals, Journals & Planners, specially crafted for women of color. Our collection resonates with the unique journeys, dreams, and aspirations of every vibrant woman out there. MeEvolv Devotionals, Journals and Planners are crafted with precision and passion, our collection is designed to guide you through every step of your evolution. Whether you're setting goals, tracking progress, or simply seeking clarity, MeEvolv is your companion in the quest for a better you. Dive deep into self-reflection, plan your days with purpose, and watch yourself evolve. Continue your journey with MeEvolv today.

Visit www.MeEvolv.com for a full list of our products.

Harnessing Confidence Through Self-Care